Called Out by God

Know Your Rank and Mission

Kent Simpson, Prophetic Pastor

Copyright © 2014 by Kent Simpson, Prophetic Pastor

Called Out by God
Know Your Rank and Mission
by Kent Simpson, Prophetic Pastor

Printed in the United States of America

ISBN 9781498420563

All rights reserved solely by the author. The author guarantees all contents are original and do not infringe upon the legal rights of any other person or work. No part of this book may be reproduced in any form without the permission of the author. The views expressed in this book are not necessarily those of the publisher.

Scripture quotations taken from the New King James Version (NKJV). Copyright © 1979, 1980, 1982 by Thomas Nelson, Inc. Used by permission. All rights reserved.

www.xulonpress.com

Endorsement

Kent Simpson's CALLED OUT BY GOD is for EVERY BELIEVER TODAY and it should also be in ever New Believer's Class and "required reading" in every Bible College "Christianity 101" class. There is a lifetime of teaching in this book that will stir up the hearts, minds and even the gifts within every Believer who takes it seriously.

I've known Kent Simpson, as a prophet and as a friend, for almost 25 years and in all those years, he has never disappointed me when he writes— he always invigorates my mind with what the Scriptures teach—truths to benefit me— that I had often overlooked. In the same way, in this book, Kent will have you asking, again and again, "Does the Bible really teach that for Believers today?" And again and again, you will discover that the Bible DOES teach what Kent says it does.

New Believers, college students, and like me, long-time believers will be inspired and refocused on what it means to walk out and work out "your salvation with fear and trembling." Some of the most SIMPLE BUT OVERLOOKED teachings and truths in the Church today for the Body of Christ are clearly laid out in this book. Believers worldwide need to be reminded what it means when you are "CALLED OUT BY GOD."

This is simply a MUST-HAVE book for every Christian today. Get one for yourself and one for a friend, I'd say!

Steve Shultz, Founder, THE ELIJAH LIST

Table of Contents

Chapter–1
How to Know the Signs from God 15
- Will you go AWOL or will you serve? 15

Chapter–2
Pulling Down Strongholds 20
- If God Does Not Speak Then Shut UP! 20
- It's all about Attitude 21
- Terrestrial Christians vs. Celestial Christians 23
- Our Weapons for Spiritual Warfare 26
- Weapons of a Celestial Christian 27

Chapter–3
What is Your Rank in God's Army? 28
- Know Your Rank and Mission 28

- Amputated from the Body of Christ 29
- Battle Hardened Christians vs. Bench Warmers 30
- What is Most Important to Jesus? 31
- Jesus is the Word of God 33
- You Can Only Serve One Master 35
- All Ranks in God's Army are NOT Equal 36
- What does it Cost to Serve the Almighty One 37

Chapter- 4
Abiding in God's Will 39
- The Deep Calls unto the Deep 40
- Who or What is the Word of God 41

Chapter 5 –
Your Purpose, The Process, His Promise 44
- Your Purpose and New Identity 44
- The Process, Baptism of Fire 47
- His Promises Will Come to Pass IF... 52

Chapter 6–
Your Prophetic Word Confirmed 54
- Sons of Thunder 54
- Learning by the Example of Others 55

Table of Contents

- The Key to Finding Your Purpose 57
- Getting Started is the Hardest Part 58
- Being Loyal to the Commission 59
- What Will God Do for You? 60
- What is the Most Important to You? 60

Chapter– 7
Knowing the God's Will 62
- Know His Voice 62
- Anointing by Association 63
- God's Knowledge vs. Human Reasoning 63
- Knowing All Things by the Spirit 66
- Jesus Prophesied and Imparted Gifts 67
- Down the Hallway to the Promise of God 68

Chapter- 8
Angels, what are they for? 72
- Jesus and His Angels 72
- Ministering Spirits to Minister FOR Us 77
- Angelic Presence Make All the Difference 81

My Editor

Without the help of my lovely daughter, Jenny I would not have been able to tackle this project. She has been a teacher and exhorter to her old Dad who sometimes does not pay too much attention to details. However, being she faces a class room of high school students each day she more or less accustomed to there being a lack of attention.

Jenny and I plan on doing a number of other projects with the help of a few special friends. There will be finer works coming out as I slowly learn from my editor how to express my thoughts into the text format. Bless you my daughter for being so patient to your old Dad.

Forward

The Lord is sending out a powerful message to those of us who have signed up to follow Him. He is serious about how we live in these days. We can no longer pretend that there is nothing happening in the spiritual realm that we are a part of, (ready or not). This is a book of truth that prepares us to 'get ready' and then 'quickly move forward' in the work of the Kingdom of God.

It is not a time to be easily offended. God is on the move, and we are required to move with Him. It is not about us; it's about what He requires of us. Spiritual growth can happen rapidly when we are open to His leading.

Following the wise counsel that Prophet Kent Simpson has offered, is a way to see definite changes take place in a very short period of time. The message is clear, concise, and it works!

Judith Oldridge
Prophetic Elder
Prophetic Ministries Today (PMT)

Chapter- 1
How to Know the Signs from God
by, Kent Simpson

Will you go AWOL or will you serve?

Looking at what has happened in this world over the past few years, we find evidence that many times a prophetic prelude reveals how the natural world is paralleling to the world of the supernatural, and thus the prelude creates a manifesto for the Church. There are valuable prophetic signs to be gained through these natural events. The Holy Scriptures have revealed to us a way to read the signs, forecasting what is ahead of us.

"However, the spiritual is not first, but the natural, and afterward the spiritual" (1 Corinthians 15:46).

There have been hundreds of thousands of young men and women who have signed their names on the dotted line to fight in the wars in Iraq and Afghanistan. Many of them signed up for the opportunity to obtain a higher education or receive an income they could not make in the civilian world.

Many members of our military found themselves in the midst of something they did not think they signed up for, yet they served with all that was within them. Still, others signed up just to fight for what they believed in.

As these wars begin to fade away, we can see through our nation's rearview mirror that very little was accomplished if anything. What we do see is a massive loss of life, property and the demise of our lifestyles. Pondering over the peak of our nation's pain, it is clear that we became highly motivated by anger, fear, vengeance and greed. All these emotions were triggered after 9/11. So what have we learned, and what could we have done differently in order to turn tragedy into a positive mark in our nation's history? Is it possible that we could have handled this event with a heart of love rather than of hate and had victory without the loss of lives, limbs and minds and without sacrificing our best, bravest and brightest?

We now have before us a chance to redirect the destiny of all godly nations in the world. However, we must first look deeper into the sign that has been played out over the past years in order to properly forecast what direction the Holy Spirit wants to take God's people.

Now, the people of God whose names have been signed into the Book of Life are being called up to fight a different kind of war, a spiritual war. When we stood up for Jesus we may have thought we were going to get a free ride. Not so! We are now being called upon to serve in His supernatural force, fighting a much different kind of foe.

For many years prior to 9/11 we experienced peace and prosperity enjoyed the preaching and being caught up in the praise and worship and the fellowship at all the potlucks and other such events. But now, we are at a place and time where God is calling His people to unify into an army, joined together and empowered by His love. We are already seeing a manifestation of His power. There are signs that reveal we are gaining forces from within through laying down our old traditions and fears and welcoming the Holy Spirit to come in and lead His Church into this new approach to spiritual warfare. If you are in this movement of God you can easily see a surge of power being released from the Holy Spirit as it is being poured into the followers of Jesus Christ, our Lord and Savior. In the natural, we are seeing a mass exodus from non-spiritual church groups. People are being led by the Holy Spirit into the baptism of Jesus, as spoken of in Acts 19:1-7. Those who have been ministering for a number of years are experiencing a huge increase in miracles, healings, revelations of knowledge, and shocking responses to our prayers.

The Church and its leaders are not the only ones who will be on the front lines in this spiritual war. From the new born-again child of God to the oldest and most mature godly leaders, we will be mixing it up with the enemy; however, our weapons are not of this world. Like I have mentioned–this is a new approach to dealing with spiritual warfare. Looking at the errors made in the natural wars, we can learn from this sign from God as to how to obtain victory in this spiritual war against our enemies.

In the natural wars, you look at everything with your natural eye. It is much different when you are involved in spiritual wars; to be honest, most of the past spiritual battles the church has been through have not been so successful and I am about to tell you why. Our enemy cannot be viewed as a human or a foreign nation.

"For we do not wrestle against flesh and blood, but against principalities, against powers, against the rulers of the darkness of this age, against spiritual hosts of wickedness in the heavenly places" (Ephesians 6:12).

There is one reason why so many of the church's battles never seem to be victorious. Some battles have been over such topics as abortion, same sex marriage, serving in the military, violence on television and video games, and a number of other saber-rattling convictions the church has cried out against. I could take them one by one and go into great detail, but let me just try to give you the gist of why our methods have not worked.

Chapter 2
Pulling Down Strongholds

If God Does Not Speak Then Shut UP!

*F*irst and foremost, greatest problem within the church is that the mainstream or majority of the body of Christ does not believe anyone can really talk to God and receive a clear answer or direction. This ignorance reveals that many within the mainstream do not believe what is written in the Bible, for everything in the Bible is about hearing God. Without consulting our heavenly Father about what we should do, someone starts a battle cry against a group or issue. They get the idea that all Christians don't like what is happening in the world and, on their own, they decide to declare war. If you are not going to seek God for His approval to go to war over any issue you will always lose, because you will not have His Word to back you!

It's all about Attitude

The second thing that has kept the Body of Christ from being victors in the eyes of the world and our heavenly Father is our attitude. The Church should not be the manic macho group that goes around condemning and judging the world. We are NOT called to judge the ways of the world. The commandments from our Lord are very clearly stated; for we are not of it and we are not to rule over it. It belongs to a different ruler, Satan himself. In Jesus' own words He commands His Church, "Therefore be merciful, just as your Father also is merciful. Judge not, and you shall not be judged. Condemn not, and you shall not be condemned. Forgive, and you will be forgiven" (Luke 6: 36 & 37). We are not called to judge the world; however, we are to hold only those of us in the church accountable to what is right and just in the eyes of God according to His word. "And if anyone hears My words and does not believe, I do not judge him; for I did not come to judge the world but to save the world" (John 14:47). It pays to obey the convictions within our heart, even when we do not think we have done anything wrong, for it is the Holy Spirit who is judging us. Therefore, we need to pray the prayer of forgiveness.

"When we are judged, we are chastened by the Lord, that we may not be condemned with the world" (1 Corinthians 11:32).

On the other hand, we are to judge ourselves, also those who are in the body of Christ. The protocol for how to judge other believers is very clear. The biblical order for having someone's inappropriate lifestyles or heinous actions judged and dealt with can be found in Matthew 18:15-20. There are leaders within the body of Christ who are anointed and chosen by our Lord who have the power to make final judgments within the Body of Christ. Jesus commissions His disciples in John 21:23, "'Peace to you! As the Father has sent Me, I also send you.' And when He had said this, He breathed on *them,* and said to them, 'Receive the Holy Spirit. If you forgive the sins of any, they are forgiven them; if you retain the *sins* of any, they are retained.'"

We even see in scripture where God empowered leaders who demonstrated their power in 1 Timothy 1:15-20 by enforcing the commandment on earth as it was declared in heaven. There are proper settings for governing the Church established and ordained by God. There is an order for handling individuals or groups of believers according to these scriptures and their examples.

Terrestrial Christians vs. Celestial Christians

ID of the Terrestrial Christian: one who is born-again and saved from eternal damnation and baptized in the baptism of repentance. They have a form of godliness but are "unloving, unforgiving, slanderers, without self-control, brutal, despisers of good, traitors, headstrong, haughty, lovers of pleasure rather than lovers of God, having a form of godliness but denying the power" (2 Timothy 3:3&4). Not believing in the Baptism of the Holy Spirit or that spiritual gifts are for today. These types of Christians rarely help the church and seem to enjoy coming against everyone outside of their own congregations.

ID of the Celestial Christians: Christians who have been born again, saved from eternal damnation, baptized in water, the baptism of repentance, also known as the baptism of John the Baptist. These Christians have also been empowered by the baptism of the Holy Spirit, also known as the baptism of Jesus Christ.

Not all Christians are the same and we are not all equal. How could we think that we all have received from God the same blessings, beauty, intelligence, humor, talents and even spiritual gifts? Life is not fair and we are not all equal. Although, it sounds good to tell everyone they are all equal and you have been told at some point that God has no favorites. Well, then what about King David, a man after God's own heart, and his son Solomon the richest man in the world in his day and forevermore, as recorded in the Bible? What matters to God is what you do with all that He has given you in this life.

You may be living the most horrible life one can imagine. If so, I encourage you to be an overcomer and stretch yourself to do more than anyone expects you to do, and even God will notice and reward you.

We are rewarded by what we do, not by who we are. Your eternal blessing could be the greatest in all of heaven depending on what you do with what God gave you while you were on this earth. Jesus has told us, "Take heed what you hear. With the same measure you use, it will be measured to you; and to you who hear, more will be given" (Mark 4:24).

You see, it's easy to begin climbing out of your slump, depression, financial problems, health problems and whatever else that is holding you down. All you have to do is pray, hear and obey, and with this one principle you will receive life more abundant as Jesus promised in this life as well as the life to come (see John 1:10b). If you do all that the Lord asks of you He will continue to reward you even when all others reject you.

> *"There are* also celestial bodies and terrestrial bodies; but the glory of the celestial *is* one, and the *glory* of the terrestrial *is* another. T*here is* one glory of the sun, another glory of the moon, and another glory of the stars; for *one* star differs from *another* star in glory" (1 Corinthians 15:40-41).

You might think of yourself as small or insignificant, but remember **you are a very** important part of God's plan for His Church. If you are a Celestial Christian, you will follow the call of God upon your life and the church will prosper because of you. The body is only 100% when all the members are operating in unity, synced together by the power of God's love for this lost and self-destructing world.

Our Weapons for Spiritual Warfare

Maybe you remember the day in Iraq when our troops and allies entered Baghdad; it was considered a major victory. In the natural realm this would be true; however, looking at the spiritual side, the victory was when our troops tied a cable around the statue of Saddam Hessian and toppled it to the ground. This was a sign from God that we too will be taking down idols and major strongholds that stand against the Son of God. The Holy Spirit is increasing our power and distributing His weapons of warfare to knock down wicked idols and not just in the natural. He is going to start knocking down idols even in your own homes.

Our weapons are listed in 1 Corinthians 12:1-11, the nine spiritual gifts of the Holy Spirit, and in Romans 12:3-8 which lists various ministries afforded to us to accomplish God's will, to win the battle against the devil who comes to steal, kill and destroy (John 10:10). We sharpen our weapons and train daily to perfect a LOVE for the lost souls by practicing these nine acts of God, which give us the power of the Holy Spirit to win over the sinner. The sinner will always be controlled by the devil and will win in any conflict when you try to use their weapons of warfare. We can never win any battle when we try to use the devil's weapons; anger, vengeance, boasting, fighting, swearing, killing, destroying, mocking or murdering and say we are serving God **are truly Terrestrial Christians.**

Weapons of a Celestial Christian

"But the fruit of the Spirit is love, joy, peace, longsuffering, kindness, goodness, faithfulness gentleness, self-control. Against such there is no law and those *who are* Christ's have crucified the flesh with its passions and desires" (Galatians 5:22-24). With the gifts, power, fruit and calling upon our individual lives we can turn this old world back to its rightful owners, God the Father, God the Son and God the Holy Spirit.

"If your enemy is hungry, give him bread to eat;

And if he is thirsty, give him water to drink; for

so you will heap coals of fire on his head, And the

Lord will reward you" (Proverbs 25:21 & 22).

Chapter- 3
What is Your Rank in God's Army?

Know Your Rank and Mission

*F*or many years now I have heard evangelists cry out to whoever would listen, "You need to know Jesus Christ as your Lord and Savior." I must say the word for today is; "You need to know that Jesus Christ knows who you are." You need to know your rank, your file, your position, which outfit you are joined up with and know what you are to do when the devil sends emotional mortars into your happy camp. It is time to get ready for a war. And this war will determine who is willing to live and die for Christ and His people.

Amputated from the Body of Christ

Over the past few centuries various men have felt the need to take control of the church and shape it into what they think it should look like. In their plan they started with changing the church government, setting it up to where they could be in control of all the functions within the congregations. Whether they controlled it as the pastor or as the chief elder or a wealthy congregational member, they were manipulating the church to fit their needs and desires.

Nowhere in the Bible do we find Jesus telling anyone to go to church, for if you are one of His then you are the church. From the Bible we can easily see that the present church government looks nothing like what our Lord has mapped out in the Bible. Early on we see that those who wanted to control the church first had to make a list of what would be accepted and what had to go; including what books and letters would be placed in the Bible. As the process continued, the leaders began amputating certain ministers and ministries from the body of believers. Moving forward, they made many political changes dictating how the church services were to be conducted.

Slowly almost all the gifts of the Holy Spirit were forbidden, and then came the amputation of the five-fold ministry, except one (Ref. Ephesians 4:11). It is as though they had planned to slowly mutilate the body of Christ by removing the arms, the ears, the eyes and feet; you get the picture. All that is left is the navel and not much happens there. Dissecting the church left it almost powerless by forbidding anyone to operate in the gifts of the Holy Spirit (Ref. 1 Corinthians 12:1-10). No squinty-eyed prophets were allowed in the building for they may reveal the heresy that has been committed before God and His people. Only outside of the walled fortress of their sacred buildings could the prophets speak. However, you need not despair, for in the past few decades the Holy Spirit has been busy **re-attaching** these lost members like spiritual prosthesis. The Spirit of God is transplanting back into the church the delicate and gifted organs, equipping this once dysfunctional body of believers to a ready Bride of Christ (ref. Matthew 25:1-13).

Battle Hardened Christians vs. Bench Warmers

Where are you being commissioned to enlist so that you may have the freedom to serve our Lord in the manner in which you were predestined? So many people are being called to serve in God's army, but they do not fit in their local church.

We are looking more like a band of rag-tag, blood-bought soldiers. We are the elect of God and look nothing like the religious bunch who have a form of godliness but deny the Holy Spirit's authority over the Church. They portray a theology of doubt and give great concern for what the world thinks about them while not giving much concern about God's thoughts. We are not responsible for them or their lukewarm attitude. As long as we are doing what the Holy Spirit is telling us to do, **then** we are protected. We cannot be in any safer place than in His will.

"We know that whoever is born of God does not sin; but he who has been born of God keeps himself, and the wicked one does not touch him. We know that we are of God, and the whole world lies *under the sway of* the wicked one" (1 John 5:18-19).

What is Most Important to Jesus?

First, we must go to the Holy Scriptures to find out what our Lord desires us to do for Him, so that we may prosper as His kingdom prospers. What the Scriptures reveal is that Jesus wanted His disciples, as well as all of us, to obey the voice of His Father (Ref. Matthew 16:13-19). Jesus repeatedly demonstrates in the Bible that He first prayed to His Father, and then He either spoke or acted according to what His Father revealed. This is the first and only thing you must do to find God's will for you and His purpose for your life. This is why our slogan is: "Pray, Hear and Obey, for it is the Christian way."

The only way to be righteous is to be right with God, and the only way to be right with Him is to do whatever He says you are to do and say. Jesus Himself said; "For I have not spoken on My own *authority;* but the Father who sent Me gave Me a command, what I should say and what I should speak. And I know that His command is everlasting life. Therefore, whatever I speak, just as the Father has told Me, so I speak" (John 12:49, 50). Therefore, who are we to think that we should do it any differently? I love to read and study my Bible. God often speaks to me through His Book, but I do not worship the book. It is a mistake to make the book an idol before God.

Many of us have been told that we cannot know God's will without knowing the Bible, that the Bible is our guide, man's operator's manual, or that if it's not in the Bible it's not from God. The adage I most often hear is the only way you can know

God's will is to read your Bible. All of these statements carry some truth, but they also teach us something that Jesus never intended. Here is what Jesus has to say about the Bible, "You search the Scriptures, for in them you think you have eternal life; and these are they which testify of Me. But you are not willing to come to Me that you may have life" (John 5:39, 40).

Jesus is the Word of God

"I am your fellow servant, and of your brethren who have the testimony of Jesus. Worship God! For the testimony of Jesus is the spirit of prophecy." (Revelation 19:13)

Let's take a look at how much value Jesus placed upon hearing the word of God. He is not talking about reading from the Bible. It is written, "Then His mother and brothers came to Him, and could not approach Him because of the crowd. And it was told Him by some, who said, 'Your mother and Your brothers are standing outside, desiring to see You.' But He answered and said to them, 'My mother and My brothers are these who hear the word of God and do it'" (*Luke 8:19-21*). Jesus is saying that his family is composed of those who hear

God and obey. Those who follow the Holy Spirit are called out by the voice of God. Those who will obediently march into whatever battle He sends them to deliver His Word. This was an important message that Jesus wanted to convey to his disciples and to us today.

When Jesus commanded His disciples to eat of his flesh and to drink of his blood, thousands of followers left him. Can you imagine how shocked they were? **It's not enough to hear His voice, but you must also know what he means.** He then turned to his disciples and asked if they were going to leave him too, but they had no place to go because they had given Him everything they had (Ref. John 6:43-58, 60-68). That is the place we all need to be. Give Him your all until there is no place else to go. Jesus is the only way; so go to our Father in prayer and do whatever He commands you say or do; for obedience is far better than your sacrifice.

> "So Samuel said, 'Has the Lord *as great* delight in burnt offerings and sacrifices, as in obeying the voice of the Lord? Behold, <u>to obey is better than sacrifice</u>, *And* to heed than the fat of rams'" (1 Samuel 15:22).

Here is one more scripture from the Bible you may have missed. "And it happened, as He spoke these things, that a certain woman from the crowd raised her voice and said to Him, 'Blessed is the womb that bore You, and the breasts which nursed You!' But He said, 'More than that, blessed are those who hear the word of God and keep it!'" (*Luke 11:27-28*).

You Can Only Serve One Master

Jesus is alive and speaking to you and me. It is not important which group you are a part of; however, who you are listening to and obeying can be a life or death issue. We have one king, one leader, one captain, one head of the body of believers, and it is Jesus Christ. He is the one who will lead us by his word into the battle. It is not about whether we will go or not go. It is how we will go. We will either submit unto his word or reject Him. Remember, He chastens those who are His. (Ref. Hebrews 12:6-8) Therefore, we will go if that is His will. He will not have a spoiled church. He will not tolerate brats in His kingdom. He wants a fit army. He wants a people who are committed to their calling.

The kingdom of God is NOT a democracy. It is a "triarchy" consisting of God the Father, God the Son and God the Holy

Spirit. It starts with the trinity and comes down through the ranks of the church. Nobody comes from below and moves up ahead. Oh, you can move yourself up from the church's lowest position to the senior pastor but if you are not called and anointed of God for the job, you and everyone around you will be miserable. You cannot move out of your position until you are told by God and it is confirmed by others. We are the body of Christ and we need to find out where we fit in His body. We need to know what our spiritual gifts are and how to use them. We need to know what we are called to do and where we are commissioned to work within the ministry that He has anointed us individually to oversee.

All Ranks in God's Army are NOT Equal

Most people think we are all equal. In the kingdom of Heaven there are different layers of authority. There are commanders, generals, and privates. What you do in this life will determine where you sit for eternity. If you are willing to serve the Lord and His people in the ministry He has entrusted to **you, then** do it to the best of your ability. My earthly father told me many times; "A job worth doing is worth doing right." How you do your job for Jesus on earth will determine how high up you will sit with Him in heaven and that is forever. Whatever your job is when you get to heaven, your mansion and surroundings will be much greater than any mansion or position that the world could ever offer. Even to sweep heaven's streets and polish the pearly gates is far greater than the most honorable job in the world. We are talking about eternity here; no one gets laid off in heaven, and the retirement benefits are out of this world!

What does it Cost to Serve the Almighty One?

We are talking about surrendering and submitting to the King of kings. This is about being led by a Spirit you cannot touch but who can touch you. You must be willing to die to your flesh until your spirit cries out "Abba Father." Then you know in your "knower" you are ready to do all that He asks of you. Your heart must be sold out to God in order to know what your marching orders are on a daily basis.

> "For as many as are led by the Spirit of God, these are sons of God. For you did not receive the spirit of bondage again to fear, but you received the Spirit of adoption by whom we cry out, 'Abba, Father.' The Spirit Himself bears

witness with our spirit that we are children of God" (Romans 8:14-16).

Regardless of reputation, regardless of what others may say or think of you, God is going to put you in a place where you will come face to face with the devil. The word of the devil may come from an in-law, a close friend, or somebody at work, but be reassured that God will put you in a place of decision. Will you pronounce Jesus as your Savior? Will you confess Jesus as your Lord? Will you go to war for His Church? Are you willing to love your enemies, turn the other cheek when you are abused, minister in the nine fruits of the Spirit, lay down your life for a stranger? If you can use these weapons to fight and never be angry, hateful, or condemning you will witness the power of the Holy Spirit and see His angels do miracles before your own eyes.

Chapter- 4
Abiding in God's Will

"If you abide in Me, and My words abide in you, you will ask what you desire, and it shall be done for you" (John 15:7).

The verse of scripture has a much deeper meaning than you may think. To "abide in Me" is to live in Christ and Him in you. And you are forbidden to meditate or touch anything that is not of Him. This part of the verse is not too difficult to understand, for anything of sin should not be let in. The next part of the verse has been misunderstood for a long time by many and needs further explanation; "and My words abide in you." Here is what most people think this part of the verse is saying; if you stay away from sin and read **your bible** every day (or as often as possible), then you are abiding in His word. Therefore their belief is that the promise in this verse "you will ask what you desire, and it shall be done for you" (John 15:7b) is automatically working for every believing Christian. And when it doesn't work in their life they question their faith and the truth of **the bible.**

We must be willing to answer the call of the Holy Spirit and be willing to follow Him to the depths of our sanity. He will take **you** through various situations along this journey teaching **you** what His Words really mean. Whether it's the written word or spoken Word we must obtain understanding **for this will increase** our knowledge and with knowledge we will become much wiser.

The Deep Calls unto the Deep

Now let's give this some thought. It's not too difficult to read your bible and restrain yourself from offending God. So why doesn't every Christian receive whatever they desire; after all, the bible promises it to be so? The promise in this verse we are discussing states that "you will ask what you desire, and it shall be done for you." This is a very powerful promise and I will explain how you are to obtain this promise. The first part of this puzzle of truth must be broken down in order for us to see the prerequisites outlined within it, before we can receive the full measure of the promise and its manifestation. Allow me to stretch your faith a little and share with you what I have been taught by the Holy Spirit. The next few steps are not meant to offend but rather to help set you in a place to where you can begin walking in the fullness of the promises of God. Remember this one thing! The Holy Bible is 100% from God and is all true. Truth will always work when applied as instructed. If what you have been taught in the past is not working then it's not being taught correctly and it's time to ask the only true teacher for the correct answers. The Holy Spirit is the author and teacher that will give you all truth and nothing but the truth. Also remember **what** is written in the Holy Bible is not all there is to know about living this life as a child of God. We can continue to learn more daily from our God; for He is **NOT dead. He is alive** and is speaking to you and me.

Who or What is the Word of God

First of all the Bible is not the Word of God, Jesus Christ is the Word of God. He can speak to you through the written words found in the bible but do not be confused; He is not wood, pulp, and ink, bound in genuine leather. The Holy Scriptures are a compilation of divine events that are inscribed testimonials about God the Father, God the Son and God the Holy Spirit. When you are reading from your bible you need to know the difference **between the (logos) word and His (Rhema)** Word. Many words in the bible have more than one meaning for they originated in languages other than English. So when we read our bibles in the English translation, the same word can be used over and over as having the same meaning; however, in the original text it may have multiple meanings. If you are reading your bible and you are obtaining information as you study, you are reading the written word or you could say the (logos) word. The Holy Spirit can use any book, billboard, poster, man, woman, child and even a donkey to speak to you. There is no limit to how God can speak His (rhema) Word or to say His life giving Word. We are always looking for the life giving Word, the (rhema) Word of God. The (rhema) Word changes our lives and gives direction, heals and delivers us. Do you know what it's like to have the Holy Spirit speak His (rhema) Word to you in the very hour you need it? This is the (rhema) Word this verse is talking about, not just whatever you want to read or claim for yourself. The verse is referring to the (rhema) Word from Jesus Christ who IS the living Word in this verse. "If you abide in Me, and My words abide in you, you will ask what you desire, and it shall be done for you" (John 15:7). I hope and pray that you understand this part and use it as your spiritual compass to guide you through life. Continually keep your spiritual antennas up, ready to receive every life giving (Rhema) Word that comes to you. It is your Master, King, Lord Jesus speaking to you. Pray, hear and obey, for it is the Christian way. Amen, so be it!

Chapter 5

Your Purpose, The Process, His Promise

Your Purpose and New Identity

When our Father's abiding word is working within you, then you have found your purpose for your life, and this purpose becomes your identity. Too many believers today do not know where they fit in the Kingdom of God. One of the very first acts of every Christian should be to find out what God's purpose for them is in this life. Before we can begin to please God with our works we must first find out what His purpose is for us.

If we are not of this world, then we should not be so concerned about where we fit in it. This short time we have on earth is a time of testing to see if we are loyal subjects who will serve our Father or serve the ruler of this world, the prince of darkness (ref. Eph. 2:2). This life is training us to be prepared to endure the lengthy boot camp God has called us into.

Our Father has a three-part purpose for giving each and every one of us a word. It gives us direction on what we are called to do for His people. The word gives purpose by revealing to us how we are to go about fulfilling the work He has placed before us. He has a purpose for imparting to us **a spiritual gift** from the Holy Spirit so that we will be equipped to demonstrate His power, letting all know that we are His anointed ones for the job He has purposed for us to do.

When most of us begin to think about what we could possibly do for the Kingdom of God, we are limited in our thoughts to just a few duties found within the local congregation. You might consider being a pastor, a or praise and worship leader, a sound and technical person, a Sunday school teacher or one of the other smaller positions. We cannot limit God and keep Him locked in the box that man has created, appearing to be the only expression of His church the world will see. Our Father is much more radical than what most people may think, so do not be surprised if His word to you sounds a bit unethical and unacceptable to the religious standards many of the pious bunch hold today.

One of the most quoted verses of Scripture that most of us have either heard, or been falsely corrected by, is found in Romans 8:28, "And we know that all things work together for good to those who love God, to those who are the called according to *His* purpose." If you read this verse a couple of times you might see that there is a condition within this verse that is very important. It seems that every time things do not work out for one of our brothers or sisters we quote this verse as to say its okay. You love God, however, you are going to make mistakes or bad things are going to happen to you- that's **just the way it is. Well, I have found** that the part that makes all the difference is found in the last few words of this verse, "called according to His purpose." Now if you read this verse as it is written, then you will see that it is saying if you are in God's purpose and do all things according to His word (your calling, commission and gifting) good things will come to you and the evil one cannot touch you.

Most people think that if they are doing good things for people then they are fulfilling God's purpose, but that is simply not so. I counsel people almost every day. Many of them are doing good things in the site of the religious bunch to impress one another and God too. But their good deeds are dead works in the eyes of God leaving them an open target for Satan to mess up their lives. Now, if they are doing what our Father has commissioned them to do, then the devil cannot touch them; "he who has been born of God keeps himself, and the wicked one does not touch him" (1 John 5:18b). Or do you believe that God has no power over the devil? Let's get real here, God created ALL things and this includes Satan who has a purpose, too; remember, "He comes to steal, kill and destroy" (John 10:10). What is your purpose and what are you called, commissioned and equipped to do for our Master and Lord Jesus Christ and His Church?

The Process, Baptism of Fire

There is a process that everyone must go through before they can receive their promise. No one likes the process and some fail the test by doubting God and His word. That is why the verse says, "For many are called, but few *are* chosen" (Matthew 22:14). Not everyone is able to hold on to His word through all the obstacle courses that this boot camp has laid out to test their faith. To be in God's Army you have to be fit to endure it all until you finally come to the place where all the pain and suffering just does not matter anymore. Many make grand commitments to the Holy Spirit while standing in the midst of His Shekinah glory. It is easy to serve God when you feel as though Jesus has His hand on your shoulder. The real test comes when you are standing alone toe to toe with the devil and he is doing his best to get you to believe Satan rather than God and beating you down with doubt and disbelief. Remember these words when you are being tested in this manner: He that is in you is greater than he that is of this world. And don't doubt in darkness what you have committed to in the light. Everything will be all right, for when you have passed through the process you will reap what has been promised to you.

"He will baptize you with the Holy Spirit and **fire**" (Matthew 3:11b).

Before David was placed upon the throne, he received a word from Prophet Samuel that he would, in fact, someday become the king (ref.1 Samuel 16:1-13). Twenty years later that word came to pass, because David kept that word in his forethoughts and every time he was challenged by whatever obstacles were thrown into his path he was reminded of his purpose.

During the process David's prophetic word was put to the test. He was challenged many times when he faced the lion in the woods. David could have died. His prophecy would not have come to pass except he was reminded of God's word and promise. He could not die. He had power over the lion, because his word had not yet come to pass.

When David faced the bear, it was the same situation, but this time his faith was stronger because he survived the lion. When David took the five small stones to challenge the giant it was nothing, because his faith had already grown to the point where he knew the giant could not touch him. David believed in the word of God and fulfilled the purpose in his life.

The evil one cannot touch you if you are in the will of God. If the devil is beating you up something is wrong. You need to find out from the Lord if He wants you to be somewhere else or if you need to change what you are doing. God is holding men and women accountable today in what they say and how they lead His troops into this new battle.

"My brethren, let not many of you become teachers, knowing that we shall receive a stricter judgment" (James 3:1).

There is greater accountability for those who are in leadership, because they are accountable to God Almighty for what they tell others to do. They are accountable for your soul. This is not a picnic or a party. The Church is not another club to join. It is becoming an entity issuing fatigues and bars and stripes. It is calling out those who will fight in this spiritual war.

Remember, what you do in this life will determine your rank and position for eternity. How you lead others in this life will determine where you are placed in His chain of command. Don't let the devil give you an image of heaven with you wearing a white gown sitting on a cloud strumming a harp. That is not the Kingdom of Heaven!

Those who have gone to the other side, those who died and returned, have said it is just like earth but much, much better. Sometimes we take this life far too seriously. In reality we are too comfortable. When we begin to worship this life as greater than the one to come then it becomes difficult to find peace or hear the Prince of Peace.

When you are called out by God and His word abides in you, you have chosen to come into agreement with His word. You have saluted and marched toward the call of God, and you cannot afford to look back. A person is not fit for the kingdom of God if they put their hand to the plow and then look back.

> "But Jesus said to him, 'No one, having put his hand to the plow, and looking back, is fit for the kingdom of God'" (Luke 9:62).

Don't look to the past and lament about how things used to be. We do not serve a God of the past. He is a God of today. He is not a God who died, gave us a book, and put us in charge. God is ruling and reigning from heaven now.

Every situation and every occurrence in your life has a meaning from heaven above. In everything that happens in your life, there is a cause and effect. When unexpected things happen to you and you do not know why, you need to seek God and find out. You have a right to know and you can find out because Jesus is alive and speaking to everyone who will follow the sound of His voice.

His Promises Will Come to Pass IF...

The promises of God are very personal and are directly connected to you doing whatever He asks you to do. The more you do for Him the more He will do for you. It is like any relationship, you must be willing to give of yourself even at the most difficult of times. The devil will try and make you believe God just wants to take your life and make you a slave. Not so. In fact you will find that after you have served Him awhile and proved to Him you are loyal to do whatever He asks of you He will trust you with more and more of His power, people and resources. It is a great thing when you have finally come to the place where God starts calling you His friend. To be a friend of God is to operate in a higher covenant with Him; you find yourself in a relationship that is full of His promises.

Over the years I have witnessed people trying all kinds of weird methods in an attempt to force the promises written in the bible to come to pass for their needs. I have heard many preachers saying that we can have whatever we ask just by claiming it in the name of Jesus, as if you can use His name to cast spells. The bible is not like Aladdin's lamp. We cannot just rub it three times chanting a few verses and receive whatever we are wishing for.

To have a true friend takes a lot of effort and years of bonding. With each battle you find yourself in, you know your Friend is always right behind you backing you up. You have to want to go the distance with Jesus in order to build this type of relationship. He desires us all to be His friend; that is what He created us for. Begin building your relationship with Jesus today by asking what you can do for Him; rather than telling Him what YOU want. This is the KEY that unlocks the door to the abundant life He promised you and me.

> "Then He said to them, "Take heed what you hear. With the same measure you use, it will be measured to you; and to you who hear, more will be given" (Mark 4:24)

Chapter 6

Your Prophetic Word Confirmed

Sons of Thunder

At the Mount of Transfiguration when Jesus transcended into light, Elijah and Moses appeared before Jesus, Peter, James and John. The disciples were so overwhelmed with the experience that they wanted to proclaim the place holy and build three tabernacles, one for Elijah, one for Moses and one for Jesus. Then from heaven above, the disciples heard the Father say, "This is my beloved son with whom I am well pleased. Hear him" (2 Peter 1:17b). The Father was not interested then (or now) in any building; He was only interested in his Son, the Word of God, and confirming that we hear and obey Him.

"And so **we have the prophetic word confirmed, which you do well to heed as a light that shines in a dark place**, until the day dawns and the morning star rises in your hearts" (*2 Peter 1:19*).

Peter is saying that each and every one of us has a prophetic word. The audible word of His Father was spoken over Him for all to hear. His word said He was His Son and multitudes for generations to come would hear and obey Him. What is your prophetic word? We are all commissioned and equipped to serve in His kingdom. You will be assured of your identity in Christ when you have fully died to yourself and given Him your all. When His word comes to you and you abide in it, nothing can stop you. Nothing!

Learning by the Example of Others

I had no idea what to do when I was called into ministry in July of 1976, when the Lord spoke to me from Ezekiel 33. At the very end of the chapter there is reference to being a prophet. According to my limited knowledge at that time I thought prophets were men who wore camel skin coats and had honey dripping from their beards. I thought prophets must be weird people, but I really did not know that for sure because I did not know any prophets during that time of my life. A few years later the Holy Spirit commissioned me. He revealed how I was to perform my duties by sending out prophecies through the mail.

After receiving my call to be a prophet of God, I could feel the pressure of His hand start moving me toward learning the prophetic ministry, but I was not interested. I liked my job as bank president; being highly respected in the community. My hours were great and I had something everyone wanted, money to loan. Now God wanted to humble me by making me look like a freak in the eyes of the people. I knew that my life in the spotlight would be over if I followed Him into this new way of living.

Some (like myself) do not have a choice when they are called into the ministry. They are going, either easily by listening and obeying, or through turbulent resistance. Believe me, if you resist, you will find out what it is like to live in the belly of a whale. It stinks so, please, do not choose the hard way.

After the rug was jerked out from under me and the dust had settled, I diligently started pursuing the way of a prophet.

I tried to enroll in various bible colleges, but God would not have it. I was confused and frustrated. Little did I know that the Holy Spirit would teach me what it really meant to be a prophet, all my duties and the ins and outs of the office of a prophet. I thought maybe a prophet was some old guy who got into people's faces, chewed them up one side and spit them out the other. I soon learned that is not what a true prophet of God is called to do.

The Key to Finding Your Purpose

When you finally submit to Him and vow to do whatever He wants you to do, His blessings will overtake you and bless you for years to come. If you hear God and obey, you cannot outrun His blessings. He will bless you in spite of yourself.

I was scared when God commissioned me to start offering my gift to the general public to send out prophecies through the mail with no more information than their name and address. I had no idea where this would lead me. God promised that if I made myself available as a vessel for Him to speak through, He would bless me. He said that wherever a prophecy was sent, I would reap a harvest. I was still reluctant to do it because nobody I knew was doing this type of ministry. The only thing that came close to working like this was a psychic and I did not want to be associated with that group. However, after three days of wrestling with what He wanted, I began to follow his command and make myself available as a vessel for Him to speak through.

Getting Started is the Hardest Part

For me, the most difficult step in this path of ministry was when I sent out the first prophecy on an audio-cassette tape. I thought I would only do one or two; however, the requests have not slowed down. From the time I started in November of 1989, I have sent out over 100,000 prophetic Words. At one point, I had a tiny ad in Charisma magazine. They immediately started receiving so much flak from other ministries and pastors that they wanted to cancel my ad.

God always gets what He wants. The ad continued in the magazine month after month for over five years. It was only later that I found out Charisma Magazine had anonymously requested personal prophecies for each of their office staff members. It was later reported to me that they were so touched by their individual prophecies that they unanimously decided they would NOT remove the ad from the magazine. God bless Charisma magazine for standing up for what they believe!

Being Loyal to the Commission

When you act on what God has commissioned you to do there will be battles but remember they are His battles. Whatever you need, He will make sure you have it in order to complete the job, if you keep moving in the direction He wants. He will not leave you out in the middle of the desert without a supply line coming to assist you. He will not let you be caught off-guard nor allow your enemy to sneak up behind you and stab you in the back. You cannot afford to go another day without crying out to God, telling him you will do what He asks of you.

When I started mailing out prophesies it seemed like a foolish thing to do and it was very humbling when I was asked what kind of work I did. In the beginning there seemed to be nothing to gain from doing what God asked. However, God will go to great lengths to change the hearts of the people.

What Will God Do for You?

We are now going into a new time of life in America, changed forever by the war that began September 11, 2001. Things are going to change even more in the marketplace, in business, governments and education. The church must change too. At present our Lord has our prophetic elders busy writing a new course of direction for the church's protocol and code of ethics. In accordance with what the Lord has reveal through His prophets, an effort is being made to revitalize the direction of the church to protect the body of believers and empower the body to overcome their enemies.

What is the Most Important to You?

Every revelation and every invention comes from heaven above. The devil never created anything. Every invention is a gift from God and all good gifts come from God. All you have to do in order to receive your gift is open your heart to Him and say, "God, use me however you so will." God is searching the globe looking for that one act of obedience so that He may pour out His blessing. He is not looking for sinners to punish. All sin has been appropriated through the blood of our Lord and Savior, Jesus Christ. In His name, we should do whatever the Father has called, commissioned and equipped us to do. Everything else that this life has to offer pales in comparison.

Chapter 7

Knowing the God's Will

Know His Voice

God is getting ready to allow calamity to rain down upon the nations, and this will drive people back into His church. The people will turn out in droves wanting to come back to our Lord. Isn't this what we are seeking? The one thing that we want to see is people coming into the kingdom of God. We are only in this life for a short period of time. This world is not what life is truly all about. This is just a blink in eternity. We need to make the best of it now. We cannot just search for life's higher levels of comfort. We need to look at why we are here and what we are to do.

Anointing by Association

In the prophetic ministry, there is a need to teach the same group of people over and over. The hit and miss approach for teaching how to hear God is not going to work. It is very difficult to teach people how to hear the voice of God when they do not have the prophetic anointing to draw them into His presence. It is by association that the anointing is transferred one to another. If you do not hang around prophetic people you will not get it. If you are just passing through you may get a little of it for a while, but it will wear off; you need to soak in it to really experience His prophetic anointing.

"But you have an anointing from the Holy One, and **you know all things**" (1 John 2:20).

God's Knowledge vs. Human Reasoning

When you have prayed to our Father and you know that you know in your "knower" that He has heard you, things begin to change. After God delivers you from the place you were trying to leave He will close the door and you will find yourself waiting for the new door to open. We call this place the "Hallway" and it sometimes is dark and scary in this spiritual hallway; you may want to bail, jump ship or abandon God's plan.

When you are in the "hallway" you should not make any major decisions. You must wait until you see the light coming through the door that stands open for you, move toward the light and trust God. If you will allow God to lead you, then you will find out who you are in Him. The hour has definitely come; we are going to see major changes. God has a plan and He is getting us ready for something big.

A lot of people are proclaiming that everything is great, but when it all falls apart the people who rested on those words are going to be devastated. However, there are people who are preparing for it. It is important for us to stay out of debt and try to be as financially free as we possibly can. To be a poor man is a hard thing but the worst thing is to be a poor man in debt. You may not have all the material things you desire, but at least you have zero debt. It is easier to find a morsel of spiritual bread, which is a word from God, than to keep looking every day for the stale loaf the world continues to promise.

> "It is written, 'Man shall not live by bread alone, but by every word that proceeds from the mouth of God'" (Matthew 4:4).

For years we have heard that we need to stay out of debt, yet people have wondered why. They thought everything was getting better. We must know what God wants us to do in the financial arena in order to have foresight on what we need to do for future plans. We need 20/20 foresight, not 20/20 hindsight. The only way to do that is to be in touch with the Lord and work under His anointing.

The time has come when God is telling certain people what to buy, what to sell, and when to sell and where to buy. God will begin to prosper us and take us through a time that will be very difficult. We cannot go on what the world promises; we must go with what the word of the Lord is for each and every transaction we make. He is the only bread we need. When we know what God wants us to do, then we will know peace. God's word will always test us. We are often being tested by His word; we either trust Him or trust the ways of this world.

"I am the bread of life. He who comes to Me shall never hunger, and He who believes in Me shall never thirst" (John 6:35).

Knowing All Things by the Spirit

We shall know all things by the Spirit. The things you need cannot always be successfully obtained by human knowledge. That is why God has given us the window of prayer to find answers, so we know how to obtain the things we need. If you need anything, you can find out how to get it by praying in the Spirit. When you pray, God will be faithful to send His ministering spirits (angels) to deliver His revelation knowledge of you, revealing how to obtain what you need.

> "But seek first the kingdom of God and His righteousness, and all these things shall be added to you" (Matthew 6:33).

One of the recorded events regarding angels interacting with man is found in the story of Jacob's ladder, a Sunday school teaching many of us have forgotten. This event is biblical proof that angels do co-exist between heaven and earth.

The Angels of the Lord are continually ascending and descending between heaven and earth, delivering messages to us and taking our prayers back to the throne of God. In a dream, Jacob saw angels traveling up and down a ladder that extended from God's throne to earth and back again. The angels were making way for the word of God to be delivered to Jacob while he slept. The promise of the Lord was given to Jacob during this dream and Jacob knew when he awoke that God had revealed His plan.

Jesus Prophesied and Imparted Gifts

The New Testament gives confirmation that a similar occurrence took place during the days that Jesus, the Son of Man, ministered on earth. While Jesus was ministering in the word of knowledge, He prophesied and imparted the gift of discernment into Nathaniel (John 1:49-51). Philip, from Bethsaida, found Nathaniel and told him about Jesus, who claimed to be the Messiah. Nathaniel did not believe that Jesus was the Messiah that was prophesied about in the Old Testament. When Jesus saw Nathaniel, He spoke a word of knowledge to Nathaniel, telling him that He had seen him sitting under a fig tree. Nathaniel knew there was no way that Jesus could have seen him sitting under the fig tree; thus Nathaniel believed that Jesus was the Son of God. The Lord gave Nathaniel spiritual eyes to see how Jesus knew and operated in these supernatural gifts by giving him the gift of discerning of spirits (*seeing angels*).

"Jesus answered (prophesied) and said to him (Nathaniel), 'Most assuredly, I say to you, hereafter you shall see heaven open, and the angels of God ascending and descending upon the Son of Man'" (John 1:51).

Down the Hallway to the Promise of God

In 1995, we were asked to go on television by a friend who worked at LeSea Broadcasting. Before I begin, allow me to go back a ways. I was introduced to a downtrodden pastor by another minister who had asked me if I could find God's will for his friend. This pastor of seventeen years and his wife became friends of ours after God was faithful in sharing His word and direction that day. This pastor was let go after serving his denomination all his adult life. He had no skills outside of ministry, no money and two teenage children. After being asked to move out of the parsonage they traveled from Hawaii to Fort Worth, Texas to meet with me expecting to receive a word from the Lord. While we ate dinner in a crowded restaurant, he and his wife began to tell us about all of their problems. They were destitute; they had lost everything and did not know where to go or what to do. I had a small tape recorder and a blank tape to record their prophecy.

It was not long before I received the message the Lord had for this man and his wife. The ministering spirit told me to tell them to go back to Hawaii; there would be someone there to meet them who would give them a place to live. This portion of the word was really hard to believe because Hawaii's real estate is very expensive. He was also to go on Christian television and begin to pray for people over the air. They seemed to roll their eyes in disbelief, but they realized they had nothing else to go on, so they took a leap of faith and agreed to go back to Hawaii. The pastor's friend paid for their tickets and he and his family flew back to Hawaii to find a home even though their pockets were empty. Just as God had said, to their surprise, they were met at the airport by the new pastor who had taken over his pulpit. The new pastor said they could move back into the parsonage, because he already had a home and they could live-rent free in the very place where they had lived before they were kicked out. As the pastor sat in the parsonage with his family he found himself struggling, scared and wanting to run away; he was now in the "Hallway" waiting for God to fulfill His promise.

For two weeks he worked up his courage to go to the Christian television station and see if he could get a spot on the channel. This man had no money; however, he stepped out on God's word and was given a spot. By faith, he started his weekly TV program. Within the first month he was unable to pay the expenses for his program and went off the air. He was stressed beyond measure. I did not know this, but he sent in his last $50.00 for another prophecy. Then he stepped back into the 'hallway' and waited for his prophetic word. The word he received was: "This very day things will change," along with other more personal words but the main promise was "This very day things will change."

The day he received his prophecy, he also received a phone call from the television station. The station asked if he would start up his program again, but this time he would become a paid employee working in sales for LeSea Broadcasting and his television program would cost him nothing. What a blessing it was for this family in Hawaii! The name of the program is "Prayer Line Hawaii" and we have a few of these programs on video where I appeared on his show and prophesied to callers live over the airwaves. Becoming friends with this television minister became a blessing in many ways for many years; the Holy Spirit took us through an awesome spiritual journey.

The very first time I started prophesying live over his program we had 11 people on the phones to take prophecy requests. For over 20 minutes we were only able to answer a few of the 248 phone calls that came into the station. The owners noticed right off that this was a huge boost in their local ratings. After the program was over, the owners started calling all of the ministers who had live programs airing at their studio and set it up for me prophesy to their viewers as well. I agreed and received no payment of any kind because the Lord had promised me that wherever I send out His prophetic word I would reap a harvest. Even after all these years, I still have close relationships with a number of people and churches from around the world due to allowing myself to be a vessel through which God could speak.

Chapter 8

Angels, what are they for?

Jesus and His Angels

"Do not forget to entertain strangers, for by so doing some have unwittingly entertained angels" (Hebrews 13:2).

*J*esus is not only our Lord and Savior but also our mentor and teacher. He is also our King and our example. Through His disciples, Jesus has shown us the way to move into the realm of the supernatural. It took Jesus three and a half years to show his disciples how to be used as a vessel of the Holy Spirit, to walk in the supernatural with evidence of signs and wonders following after them.

"Then Jesus said to him, 'Unless you people see signs and wonders, you will by no means believe'" (John 4:48).

He has shown us how to receive and embrace angelic encounters, which bring about miraculous interventions. Jesus did many different healings and miracles, but He did them in many different ways so that we would learn not to get stuck on religious formalities. When we say the same prayer and use the same method every time we minister, we begin to practice a religious formula, which negates what Jesus is teaching us to do.

Jesus had some very unconventional ways in which we healed. He spit in the dirt to make mud and then placed it on a blind man's eyes and they were healed. It is also written that he would spit directly on those who needed healing. You do not see these same types of ministries in operation today because it would not be socially acceptable. Jesus' actions were bold, but before He ever acted, Jesus prayed to the Father. Whatever the Father told Him to do, Jesus did. This always worked for Him 100% of the time. Jesus has demonstrated what we are to do, and He expects us to do the work of the Father.

Today we want to see 100% accuracy in our ministries and churches. The world needs to see the evidence that Jesus is not dead but alive and is working throughout the body of believers. We are all members of the body of Christ. Each of us has a function and a purpose. Each of us has a gifting, whether we are aware of it or not. The spiritual gift of the Holy Spirit is there even though we are not sure we have a gift. These gifts can lay dormant for a long time. One of the ways your spiritual gift may be activated is through prophecy and the laying on of hands.

"Do not neglect **the gift that is in you**, which **was given to you by prophecy with the laying on of the hands** of the eldership" (1 Timothy 4:14).

We need to be aware of how Jesus moved and walked. The things Jesus did were done according to the will of the Father. He said, "I do nothing on my own authority. I only speak what I hear the Father say." That is the Christian way. That is His example for us to follow. Many times Jesus would pray to find out what the Father had to say. When Jesus prayed, there were angels ascending and descending upon Him, giving Him instructions from heaven above. Jesus taught us to pray; "Thy will be done on earth as it is in heaven" means we need to find out first from heaven what needs to be done on earth (Matthew 6:10). When your angel brings you the Word of the Lord and you begin to walk in it, nothing can stop you, for the "Lord is faithful, who will establish you and guard *you* from the evil one" (2 Thessalonians 3:3).

When Jesus was born in a manger, there was a rising up of an army who came looking for Him. Every child two years old or under was to be slaughtered because King Herod heard that a King was born and Herod feared the loss of his position as a king.

An angel appeared before Joseph and Mary and warned them to leave the town. King Herod sought the life of their newborn son, Jesus. They left the city and stayed away for a number of years until an angel appeared before them again and told them it was safe to return, for King Herod was dead. This was just the beginning of many encounters with the angelic host in the ministry of Jesus Christ our Lord and Savior.

When Jesus stood before those who were to judge him, Pontius Pilate said to him, "'Do you not know that I hold your life in my hands? I can give your life or I can take it away?" Jesus replied, "Do you think that I cannot now pray to My

Father, and He will provide Me with more than twelve legions of angels?" 12,000 angels were at His disposal to defend Him (Matthew 26:53). Upon his word, these angels could have destroyed everything.

When Jesus walked into a city, people came from everywhere to seek him. Jesus did not have to advertise his presence. The people just showed up wherever He was because the angels of the Lord would go out and gather up the people.

> "But to which of the **angels** has He ever said, 'Sit at My right hand, till I make Your enemies Your footstool?' Are they **not all ministering spirits** sent forth to **minister FOR those who** will inherit salvation?" (Hebrews 1:13-14).

Jesus's angelic encounters are important to us because they are examples of how our lives should emulate the likeness of our Lord. We are not to worship or pray to angels. However, we are to ask for spiritual gifts and His ministering spirits to be sent by God to minister for us.

> "Shall we not much more readily be in subjection to the **Father of spirits** and live?" (Hebrews 12:9b).

Ministering Spirits to Minister FOR Us

Are you an heir of salvation; have you been born-again and baptized in His Holy Spirit? If you are born of the Spirit of God, then you are an heir of salvation. You will inherit eternal life and more.

Ministering spirits are angels waiting to minister for us when the circumstances are not humanly possible. There are times in our lives when it takes an angel from the Lord to get through to us. When you came into the Kingdom of God, an angel was appointed unto you (Psalms 34:7). When you gave your life to Jesus Christ, it is recorded in the Gospels that He went before the face of God and His angels and reported your name to Him so that it would be recorded in the Lamb's Book of Life. (Luke 12:8).

There are angels waiting for you to yield to the will of our Father so that He may dispatch one or more of these angels to minister for you. Do you know the type of ministry to which you are called? Each and every one of us has at least one angel appointed as a guardian to watch over us, but there are more angels to be dispatched by the word of God for the purpose of doing signs and wonders as you follow the calling that is upon your life.

When you have more than one angel ministering for you, things can get totally out of control and you will find yourself doing things that are not humanly possible. You do not have the intellect to comprehend what God will do through you as He appoints angels to minister for you. As long as you are fulfilling what you are called and commissioned to do, your angels will manifest and endorse you with signs and wonders.

How do we obtain these angels? How do we receive the appointment of these angels? If we do not pray to them or worship them, how do we get their assistance as promised to us?

It all begins with the gifts of the Holy Spirit. When you received the baptism of the Holy Spirit, there was a least one spiritual gift manifested in you. If you do not know what your gift is or how to operate within it, you can take some steps to find out what your spiritual gift is. The gift that is in you may need to be activated or stirred. Look back into the rear-view mirror of your past and see what happened during the weeks after you received the baptism of the Holy Spirit.

> "When they heard this, they were baptized in the name of the Lord Jesus. And when Paul had laid hands on them, the Holy Spirit came upon them, and they spoke with tongues and

prophesied. Now the men were about twelve in all" (Acts 19:5-7).

You might see the spiritual gift that was given to you that you may not have noticed at that time. Maybe you prayed for somebody and they were healed. Maybe you had a dream and it came to pass. Maybe you had a vision or a word burning in you for somebody and there was no relief until you were able to deliver the word to the person.

"Therefore I remind you to stir up the gift of God which is in you through the laying on of my hands" (1 Timothy 1:6).

The nine spiritual gifts of the Holy Spirit are attached and are part of the works of the angelic hosts of God. You cannot have one without the other. For you see, the angels are the ones who are doing the signs and wonders under the order of the Holy Spirit. Miracles do not manifest by your great mental efforts, self-will or human powers. No! It is the angel of the Lord who is sent to do the work of our Father, creating supernatural effects within your ministry to demonstrate His love for the people.

It should be an effortless deed to walk in the supernatural when the appointed angels show up to do the signs and wonders. There are so many references in the Bible about angels. If you were to look up all of the encounters, you would be blessed to know that angels are still here for us. There has not been much preaching or teaching about angels in the past because there is a tendency for people to misunderstand the subject.

When Peter was in prison, the congregation was praying for his release. An angel went to the prison and kicked Peter to wake him up. Peter asked who kicked him and the angel told him to get his things, and led him out of prison. Peter came to the house where they were praying for him and knocked on the door. A girl named Rhoda peeked out and saw Peter but did not let him in. Because she was overly excited she ran back to tell the others who were praying. "But they said to her, 'You are beside yourself!' Yet she kept insisting that it was so. So they said, **"It is his angel"** (Acts 12:15). Why would they say such a thing? Was it so common back then to see angels that it was not a big deal? Maybe we should be seeing one another's angels doing the word of the Lord.

"Bless the Lord, **you His angels**, Who excel in strength, **who do His word**, Heeding the **voice of His word**" (Psalms 103:20).

Angelic Presence Make All the Difference

Have you ever witnessed people getting slain in the power of God during a service? What do you think is happening? I have seen God's angels moving in our midst. Have you ever been in a praise and worship service so wonderful and glorious that it felt like someone was rubbing a feather behind the back of your neck or behind your legs? Maybe you felt goose bumps and wondered what it was. It is like angel wings touching us. The Holy Spirit is in our presence, escorted by His angelic host. The Holy Spirit is not limited.

There are many teachings on demons. People need to be well-informed of the fact that the devil is not dead either. But let me remind you when Satan fell from heaven he only took one third of the angels with him. This means we have two thirds of the angels on our side. The demons from hell are outnumbered by the Angels of God 2 to 1.

We must be willing to allow His angels to be appointed to us and to work through us. When you first received the power of God, there was something in your life that God wanted to do through you. Do not allow yourself to become sidetracked by television, movies, or music to the point where you become deaf to the things of God. Spend time talking to Him. Even your job or business can rob you of valuable time that you could have with God. These deterrents can cause you to miss out on His blessings. You could be left wandering aimlessly, not knowing where you are to go and what you are to do. It is not our ultimate goal to see how much money we can put in the bank. Our ultimate goal should be to find out what we can do for our Lord and Savior. What you do in this life will determine where you sit in eternity. Not all prayers are equal; however, if you pray the will of the Father, your prayers will be heard.

The Kingdom of God is much more than a city or nation. It is a fortress, a supernatural place filled with people with all kinds of different spiritual gifts and callings. There are different levels of authority and responsibilities. There is a life in the Kingdom of God that is greater and better than this one on earth. There is an experience you will go through but it is not an experience of pain. Jesus said, "There is no sting in death" (1 Corinthians 15:55). He will take us straight into His Kingdom. Remember that you are spirit and soul and the body profits you nothing. It is your eternal spirit and your soul that lives forever in your new spiritual body. Start learning how to wear the armor of God while you are here. Get into the battle; serve Him so that when the day comes, His rewards will be waiting for you.

The vast majority of people believe that a person can be possessed by a demon or a devil, but cringe at the thought that a God-fearing Believer could be possessed by an angel, a ministering spirit. Think about it, we know that when evil is working in a person they appear to have unbelievable power when doing evil things. After the hideous act is committed, most of the time the demon-possessed person does not remember what he or she did.

Do you think it is possible that a person could be possessed by an angel during the time they are ministering in the supernatural power of the Holy Spirit?

Amen, So be it!

Copyright © 2014. All Rights Reserved
by, PropheticMinistries.org
for permission to use any part of this issue
contact by email

Prophetic Ministries Today and Prophetic
Ministries Tabernacle
PO Box 774
Gainesville, Texas 76241-0774

www.ingramcontent.com/pod-product-compliance
Ingram Content Group UK Ltd.
Pitfield, Milton Keynes, MK11 3LW, UK
UKHW041948230426
12048UKWH00008B/198